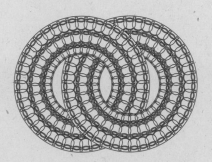

THE HISTORY HOTEL

THE

HISTORY

HOTEL

BARON

WORMSER

CavanKerry
PRESS

CavanKerry Press Ltd.
Fort Lee, New Jersey
www.cavankerrypress.org

Publisher's Cataloging-in-Publication Data
provided by Five Rainbows Cataloging Services
Names: Wormser, Baron, author.
Title: The history hotel / Baron Wormser.
Description: Fort Lee, NJ : CavanKerry Press, 2023.
Identifiers: ISBN 978-1-933880-98-3 (paperback)
Subjects: LCSH: Poetry, Modern—21st century. | Poetry. | Lyric poetry. |
    History. | Money. | BISAC: POETRY / American / General.
Classification: LCC PS3623.O76 H57 2023 (print) | LCC PS3623.O76 (ebook)
| DDC 811/.6—dc23.

Cover artwork by Janet Wormser
Cover and interior text design by Ryan Scheife, Mayfly Design
First Edition 2023, Printed in the United States of America

CAVANKERRY
PRESS

Made possible by funds from the
New Jersey State Council on the Arts, a partner
agency of the National Endowment for the Arts.

CavanKerry Press is grateful for the support it receives from the New Jersey State
Council on the Arts.

In addition, CavanKerry Press gratefully acknowledges generous emergency
support received during the COVID-19 pandemic from the following funders:

The Academy of American Poets
Community of Literary Magazines and Presses
The Mellon Foundation
National Book Foundation
New Jersey Arts and Culture Recovery Fund
New Jersey Council for the Humanities
New Jersey Economic Development Authority
Northern New Jersey Community Foundation
The Poetry Foundation
US Small Business Administration

Also by Baron Wormser

The White Words (1983)

Good Trembling (1985)

Atoms, Soul Music and other poems (1989)

When (1997)

Mulroney and Others (2000)

Teaching the Art of Poetry: The Moves
(with David Cappella, 2000)

Subject Matter (2003)

A Surge of Language: Teaching Poetry Day by Day
(with David Cappella, 2004)

Carthage (2005)

The Road Washes Out in Spring: A Poet's Memoir of
Living Off the Grid (2006)

The Poetry Life: Ten Stories (2008)

Scattered Chapters: New and Selected Poems (2008)

Impenitent Notes (2010)

Teach Us That Peace: A Novel (2013)

Unidentified Sighing Objects (2015)

Tom o' Vietnam: A Novel (2017)

Legends of the Slow Explosion (2018)

Songs from a Voice, Being the Recollections, Stanzas and
Observations of Abe Runyan, Song Writer and Performer
(2019)

Some Months in 1968: A Novel (2022)

For Janet, Maisie, and Owen

CONTENTS

III.

IV.

V.

Brief

Look! I became an old man
With wayward scraps of white hair
Sitting on a couch
In the middle of an afternoon
And writing poems in my excited
Leaves-letters-out scrawl—
Emotional errands from witless to wit
And back
Reprising Lear's journey—
Yet wonderful
In a childish childlike way
Still pecking at the mystery.

I.

Once

I was a candle
Carried upstairs downstairs
One room to another
A scholar making modest inroads
Interrogating shadows
Ardent lucid
But wavering shamefully in any draft
And untrustworthy
    firing a stray sleeve
Or curtain
My communicable sincerity a disaster

Lost and lost
   disappearing
A stub a memory
And then seemingly nothing but liable
To be reborn
    my puddled dissolution
Remelted and molded
One of the incarnated
Who supplied a modest sign
To the doubters
One who knew there was no end
To light however faint

Talk

Tell me everything you know. Then more.
I know it already but that's okay.
Repetition makes the hours grow stronger.
Information persuades and lulls,

The treadmill of declaration that can't
Go beyond a voice's imperatives.
Yes, the days fill the words, the words fly off
But return to roost on the mind's rafters

Where another set of moments will call
Them up as if they were somehow waiting,
As if what "you" say to "me,"
The long, lush, explicit reach of it,

Was foretold in a book of anti-etiquette
Or a wizard's set of instructions.

Now and then it rains money

Old coins, doubloons, heavy metal

That indents fields, ricochets off asphalt,

The hoods of cars, roofs, occasionally

A human head.

Oooh, wooh, ooof, poof

Go the money sounds.

Some people wear hats.

Some people carry baseball mitts.

Some people look up too much and fall down.

"Watch where you're going."

"Money isn't everything."

"That old stuff is worthless."

The weatherman on television is embarrassed.

There is no accurate forecast.

There is no real explanation.

There is no map he can draw.

He decides to ignore the whole thing.

People bite into the coins to make sure.

They could be counterfeit.

Reality always suggests a counterreality.

After a while the money just lies there.

Children pick it up and then throw it away.

Ode to the Stock Exchange

Ever since I was a boy the photos of guys—
    Always guys when I was a boy—
Waving their hands, clutching pieces of paper,
    Peering up at something not in the photo but
That I knew was not heaven but something

Patently human, though Tom Mussman, the atheist
    In my eighth-grade class, insisted heaven was
Very much a human invention, another in a long list
    Of categorical duplicities, not unlike the stock
Exchange where permanent excitement over fractions

Ruled so-called grown men, everyone jostling, sweaty,
    Pulling at their collars, yelling the names of money
Though that subject never came up amid the civics
    Debates, grammar drills, geography quizzes, thus
Leading me to make inferences that in these febrile

Photos lay the planet's throbbing heart,
    That this was why continents were looted, wars pursued,
And peoples subjected, that the earth was the cash
    Machine of the universe awaiting travelers from
Other galaxies in need of a loan, in need

Of regulated frenzy that went up and down like my dick
    When I pondered the breasts straining against
The blouses the girls wore in that eighth grade
    And I wondered how much anything
Could cost when its value was inestimable.

NFL Poem (Annals of Male Americana)

Late afternoon, the violet-gray gloaming,
The cars pointing home from the stadiums.
The shouts disperse. No further thrills to palpate.
Autumn is a fall. Hope has been thrown.

Stuck in such traffic, drumming the dashboard
While the work week beckons—a sickly grin
Of dull comportment. The Sabbath's air deflates
While players crow or tend their broken bones:

All in a day as dusk becomes pure night.
Paned lights grimace. Where is my warm wife?
Where are the kids? Oh! They were tackled
Or intercepted. The dark. The wrong team won.

Counting

Several air conditioners   and refrigerators
One Amana
A dozen or so automobiles
Three marriages
Love coming and going
Job transfers   all over the Midwest
How many toasters?
Two daughters
Little feet coming down the stairs
Mornings   black coffee
Moral dilemmas of childhood
None in adulthood
The fog of privacy
Voting sometimes
Rhetorical dismissals of politicians
Drinks
A handful of tears
Love coming and going
Mornings   hard to get enough
Dreams disappearing
Self-satisfaction
Aspirin
Recriminations   arguments
Absence
A favorite paint-stained sweatshirt
Birds   many birds
Blessing the sky

The New Wave

We talked about a Godard movie
My Life to Live as we ambled from
The theater to the formerly working-class
Irish bar that featured photos of Yeats

And Michael Collins, our words analyzing
What we took to be a crux of existential
Crisis rendered in a faux-documentarian style,
Such mildly acute thoughts leading to a booth

Replete with carved initials—decades of restless
Hands leaving signifying marks—as if
Creating a permanent testimony to the fated
Vanishing of identity, including the film's star,

A woman born to sexually declaim and then be shot,
A doom to which we raised our allotted whiskeys.

Elegy for the Poet Adam Zagajewski

You appeared as one of the examiners.
Life, ever laggard in her assignments
But possessed of an absurd confidence,
Came up first. And last.
She curtsied; you smiled while she pulled
Out of a battered suitcase numerous
Attempts at eloquence. "Here," she said,
"Is the heart, not just a muscle." She
Winked coyly. "Here is logic." She brandished
A volume of Descartes. You winced.

In other rooms and beyond those rooms
So much was occurring that went on happily
And unhappily, indifferent to protocols,
Brimming with anemones, half-heard melodies,
Averted glances.
                    Life cleared her throat and asked if
Everything was clear. "No," you said. "Nothing
Is clear." There was then a strangely comfortable silence,
A space that might be an era, a three-score-and-ten,
Or one of those moments that lived in memory
For what seemed like forever.
                    "Thank you," you said
To Life and somewhat remarkably she thanked you back.

II.

State Song

(for JF)

If you could catch it
This would be eternity
(My friend says to me
While we're driving through
Kansas)
Like in a book
(He goes on to say)
Like a word in a book
How something big
Really big
Way bigger than anything
Gets caught in something
Pretty innocuous
Like a word
Like I said
But this (he gestures)
Is the real
Freaking deal
Bounded somewhere
But basically free
For the eye's taking
Not asking for anything
Which is how I think
Of eternity
Not wanting anything
Not happy or sad
Just like
Kansas

On a Foreseen Death, August 4, 1962

My grandmother, always glad to pass judgment
Or rake suffering over a few more coals,
Never forgetting the pogroms or her eldest brother
Disappearing forever into the Czar's army, tsk-tsked
At yet another celebrity cul-de-sac,
Here in America where wonders were served up
Like hamburgers—eat your starry fill and perish—not

That this demise especially engaged her—another
Shiksa who'd wagged it for the world—but there it was,
Fate's bleak hand on the dire engine
That drove the obscure days forward, everyone
Sure about what they were doing, though,
As usual, Grandma was wrong, cramped
And crabbed, desolation having waylaid her
On a very foreign shore where at least one
Renamed woman was showing that

She wasn't sure, waving and almost demurely
Hollering that she hadn't asked for this life she'd
Found herself in, was weary of winking at fame's
Camera but had nowhere to turn, no earth beneath her—
Nothing—something my grandmother might have
Understood and even commiserated about
With the person—yes, there was a person—in
The MM DEAD headline, in the photos and quotes
From ex-husbands, directors, and so many actors.

Dog Is My Copilot

Great God lies down behind the stage and snores,
The fabled quiddity dispersed, much as my dog
Lies down after a vigorous dog day—
Scents of imperishable earth, two meals consumed
In eighteen seconds, a vain chipmunk chase—

The snore a spiritual hum perhaps my dog hears
Because she hears what I don't, yet I sense
Is there: contentment snuffling through
Each porous atom of the philosopher's stone,
Dreams of past times, dreams of the Great Bone

That might daunt an arduous biped
Who, sans nose and tail, can't share, despite
His inquiries, a dog's heedless, well-earned sprawl,
Her feel for the world as sniffable paradise
Answering each godly doggy need.

For Raymond Lévy

American, later, randomly percipient,
I sit on the back porch listening to a catbird
And reading about Raymond Lévy, a *Résistance* fighter,
Jew, who was arrested and transported—to use
The word of choice, applicable to material, animals,
And people, though people were "human material"
In the ideological argot of the era—to Dachau.

I was not there when the Gestapo grabbed him
On the street, that sudden, vertiginous moment.
I was not there during the interrogation to see
And hear how answers were elicited, what
Species of torture was deemed requisite.
I was not there when, in a prison cell, he pondered
How short his life was going to be, how much
He had taken for granted about his days on earth,
What he would miss the most, friends he never
Would see again. One life and no more.

The catbird continues—a mewing sound but birdy.
It could be the first day on earth and is.

But for humankind the calendar beckons, replete with
Spoken certainty and fitful feelings, commands
And musings, all echoing at the same instant,
Far off and near, as Raymond leaves
The train, his legs unsteady, a final world
In front of him, his head hurting yet clear.

I was not there. I was not there. I was not there.
Almost a series of birdsong notes. Almost
A wonderment. Almost a prayer.

A Memorable Occasion: Opening the Doors

Having earlier in the prolonged evening swallowed
   some blotter acid that came in a West Coast
care package, I found myself lying beside a cornfield
   my person dew soaked but reveling in the earth's

electric embrace, full-force gravity holding what otherwise
   might go spinning off into the mystic that was so slowly
lightening, warm filaments penetrating the soft thick murk
   around me as some birds began to speak,

their sounds forming sights like those tracer flares
   I'd seen in wars on movie screens but here portending
no distress unless it was the sense of my never moving again
   my body swallowed by the enormity, the planet for once felt

in its fullness and my receiving however feebly the power
   running through each instant that dwarfed and yet lifted up
the details of this bird and that young man and asked for
   no recompense or explanation but kept turning and turning

so that even my reordered faculties could discern the calm
   majestic motion anchoring the little green shoots of corn
headed toward a sky that sang in my ears with hosannas
   much like a Hendrix solo plangent with Eros so that

I briefly raised my head in obeisance only to fall back to the ground
   that someday would be my final dissoluble chemistry,
my vatic names leaking into this vast palpable ever-going shout.

Aces

When I win, I feel a rabid glow.
Losing is a liquid blur.
Though arbitrary,
The cards do not err.

I practice feigning patience,
I sit and wait, sip Scotch—
Sip, because that's not my vice.
I'm watching:

The dealer, the hands, the faces that float
Around me—balloons of unsure emotion.
I inhale slowly—
A pensive show that totes

A false score. I'm a captive
On the far coast of compulsion.
Where else can I record fortune's
Tremors, luck's boasts?

Poetic words to dress
An elemental craving and hurt.
A furnace of righteousness,
The writer Dostoevsky earned

His losses at the evil baize tables.
Afterward, he shrieked with shame.
He loathed the vivid, impure West.
He lacked feeling for the game

Of life. Like a black Sunday,
Purity oppressed him.
Still, I salute his urge,
The drama of our giving in.

Upon the Death of the Actor Philip Seymour Hoffman from "Acute Drug Intoxication"

Don't you do it. Don't lose yourself this soon:
A lesson for a walk down Despair Street.
You might have flown past the cold of the moon,

That distance within you, that pointless tune
Your life kept humming: *an actor is incomplete.*
Don't you do it. Don't lose yourself this soon.

You enter another once-famous tomb.
The walls have sagged. There is no star to greet.
You might have flown past the cold of the moon

As try to explain your sorry self to the wound
That roved from role to role and lived on grief.
Don't you do it. Don't lose yourself this soon.

Stand beneath a balcony, hear Romeo croon
While Lear searches for a darker heath.
You might have flown past the cold of the moon

Where no final lines conspire with stormy swoons:
Eloquence throbs with blood's bleak heat.
Don't you do it. Don't lose yourself this soon.
You might have flown past the cold of the moon.

Reasons of State

Here is the murdered child.
Here is the murdered mother
And another and another.

Here are the reasons of state.
Here is the leader who
Severely gesticulates,

Invents necessities,
While history pouts and yawns—
More blood for more treaties.

They were crossing a street.
They were fleeing to elsewhere.
They held hands. "My sweet,"

The mother said, "hold tight."
Here are the reasons of state:
Someone barks—you fight.

Books are full of this.
But not the child or mother
Or another and another.

Sentence

after Gwendolyn Brooks

Easy to wake, enjoy this day where someone named "I"
Goes forth to smell flowers, drive a car, swear
At some small annoyance while wondering how to
Hold this day not just in present-tense focus but keep
The past of it there, the grit in history's pipes, the
Fear beneath the bed and school and office where the dead
Can be heard faintly rattling bones, spitting upon
The presumptions of persons who think (or wish) that my
Life has no shadows, who say to death "never mind."

III.

Selfie

After taking a picture of herself
Nude, standing up, to send
To her boyfriend, she started crying—
Pleasure and pride dissolving
In the instant glow, the pang of me / not me
Exploding, grief for what lay inside,
Unphotographed yet leading
Its own stark life that wanted to be seen—
Her soul-sense—but never would
Or could, her revealed beauty blocking
A deep, unuttered magnificence—
Perhaps what he adored even
More than the breasts and thatch of hair
And winsome, sixteen-year-old smile,
All that stood within her given name
And that a year later would entice
Random World-Wide-Web-comers,
This body blazing forth the call
Of one love, the many betrayals.

Night, Apartment Towers, Manhattan

(for JMB)

With each lit window the premise of a life,
Presenting to the arcane, oneiric,
Restless romantic pursued and harassed by
Glib daytime—thick with money, pigeons,
Litter, the wrapping and unwrapping, need and want
Circling, the air above the subway grates
Visibly, slowly swaying—presenting then
A vision blessed by nighttime and proffering
An ever-eyed show of cozy geometries,
Serried beacons to each mind-flung
Pedestrian who looks up, not at the fuddled,
Barely to-be-seen firmament but this fabric
Of steady warmth, metered electrical magic,
Each portal a realized promise:
What might lie within, what shared,
And what must be intoned in a spasm
Of love, rhetoric, longing, and anguish—"home."

Two Painters

    1. Hopperesque

Entities—houses, storefronts, coffee cups, gas pumps—
Irremediably *there*, fulfilled by light
Except for the strangeness of his people, their pale flesh
Refusing the steady modest blessing, their souls unlit,

Preferring the hazards of purpose, whether sitting on a bed
Or passing time in a diner or doing something at those gas pumps
Whether with another person or not, all the same;
The strangeness translating into inherent aloneness,

Almost a curse if such people were attuned to curses
But still participating in the grandeur (as the painter knew)
Even if they could not help their precarious selves,
Even if you went to ask a question and they would blink

And slowly mouth, "What? What did you say?" as if aroused
From a fairy-tale sleep, a death-in-life that went on living,
Lifting cup to lips, staring at something beyond any horizon,
Making the smallest of talk, each syllable

A leaf falling from an already bare tree and never reaching
Anything solid as earth while the musical light,
A volcanic agonist drunk on heat and gas, infinity's motes,
And cosmically good for everything, played on.

2. John Singer Sargent

They—the daughters and wives of directors of boards,
Various official and unofficial aristocrats,
Some scholars of taste, small platoons of academicians,
And a pittance of raffish bohemian idlers—
Spoke for beauty—a bereft commodity,
A negligent scarf stuffed in the valise of money
Though not so much an afterthought or whim
As an adornment best requisitioned
From the throne of antiquity—the Grecian urn,
Chinese porcelain, Japanese screen
That needed no contemporary validity.

An era that could buy up other eras
While an occasional painter took the fine measure
Of what? A vagrant life, technique's raptures,
The easel's stolid murmur, nods at transience—
Children, street scenes, a bowl of fruit—all
The same, beauty's terrors being hidden,
The depth beneath the beguiling sheen, time's
Stoppage though not death. Something ever elsewhere,
A tingle and presentiment and then—there!—
In that mélange of colors in the guise
Of immemorial moments, more feeling than any deft
Hand had the right to touch if not to grasp.

1910

(for AG)

The somnolent, greedy nations do not ruin
  the known world.
Amedeo and Anna, heady with affinity, stroll
  amid the Luxembourg Gardens, pausing
  when their rapt pulses dictate.

Lenin gives up his rhetoric to raise orchids.
Trotsky turns to the Kabbalah and ponders the wisdom of mystery.
Capitalists renounce their riches to become mendicants.

The spiritual, as evinced in the paintings of Amedeo and poems
  of Anna, dwells unthreatened, borderless.

Progress spends years on a haiku.
Scientists do not cut down the tree of knowledge.
Electric excitement sits each drowsy afternoon with a glass
  of aged Burgundy.
Cannons are for small children to climb on.
Horses snort peaceably at the occasional, eccentric car.

Amedeo finds the money for more paint, Anna for ink.
Neither the colors nor the words will fade: they know this.

Lovers sit on benches surrounded by other lovers,
  their fates unencumbered by pistols and flags.
Like confetti, treaties are tossed out second-story windows
  after a night of reveling: death to all dire solemnity.

The Americans do not have to become lost.
The Russians do not have to become Soviet.
Amedeo and Anna kiss, not chastely, but full on,
  importunate, love's spendthrift license.

Venus Aligned with Mars

1.

Love boasted: so many liaisons in her
Vainglorious name, so much ill-requited fame.
An army marched through, raping, killing, maiming.
The men shot dogs for the sport of it,
Wrote letters home to sweethearts proclaiming
In uncensored terms their amative arts.

Better then to ignore such planets,
To wish for an ascetic breeze
And prate of peace, the war between the sexes done,
Battlefield attendants picking up
Bouquets and bullets, exquisite shattered cups.

2.

A chaplain who'd visited a whore
The night before picked up the Good Book
For another self-condemning look.
Life went by—a concupiscent, spiritual chore.

Writers of romances stewed in the stupor of desire:
Winks and glances jousting for diminished ends.
The lieutenant and the coquette made a pyre
Of their passion. Better than ending up as friends.

A demagogue, vexed over the lack of salt
In his soup, slapped his slovenly wife:
Take that and that and that.
Love boasted but who loved her back?

A Certain Teacher Does Some Banking

(for DC)

The teacher has some heavy minutes he wants to deposit.
"Not the light ones that evaporate," he explains
   to the teller.
"Not the ones that suggest life is not so corporeal,
   that seconds are instances of nothing.
Not those."

The teller nods, smiles politely.
All in a day's work.

"I mean," the teacher goes on, "the ones from childhood
Where you are shamed or you glimpse your parents
Having sex, not necessarily with one another.
Or you lose your car keys or your girlfriend or your savings."

"Not here," the teller replies. "Savings here are guaranteed
   by the government."

The teacher brightens up. "Resentment? Do you guarantee that?
Self-doubt? Feckless longing?"
His voice is rising.

"Just tell me your minutes," the teller insists, "but do it now.
There are people in line behind you."

The teacher turns around.
A line stretches out the door and down the street.
Some people have sleeping bags and cots.
Someone is grilling fish on a small hibachi.
Others play cards.

The teller clears her throat but the teacher feels an awe
   that goes beyond words.
He stutters. "I don't need my minutes.
My minutes aren't mine." He bows. The teller bows back
Then says, "Next."

The Shuffle

Lost my soul in the shuffle.
Got a self instead.

Not a fair deal, not even-Steven,
Not Roger-dodger.
Moped. Nattered. Felt half-dead,
Though why did such fey items matter?
Wasn't a turnip or baseball or tree.

Couldn't trade it for a car,
Though, in the legends before cars,
Various shifty characters
Swapped souls for knowledge
And temporal power.

                           Over centuries
The terms of the game change.
Centuries do that. Scour. Wipe.
You might as well contend with oblivion.

Still, there's that lingering longing,
The cry of the inner sea,
The housing of infinity.

IV.

And You, Thomas Hardy

Rain on the cemetery
The granite bereft
A thin strident wail
For bright days

Excursions to the shore
Exuberant anniversaries
A red dress or bow tie
The lies a person

Tells to age
Chatter before
The closed door of perpetuity
The rain continuing

People picnicking
Amid the headstones
Couples coupling
That ineradicable sound

That used to spook
The caretaker but which
He no longer hears
His steps grown deaf

Two Songs

1. Outtake from *Cymbeline*

Time has stowed away
  Better cargo than you.
To seek a sly way out
Only makes for clever pains,
  So dance in chains
And sing your doubt,

Canvass and bloviate—
  Your wretched heart can't feign.
Time will split your fate:
  Unwitting tinder
  For darker states
And ever-rueful moods.

Marry and covet and lust—
  All fleshy wealth be yours
To trumpet and discuss
But time yawns while your hours
  Turn to rust,
  Your ravings misconstrued.

Run off run close be still—
  All the wearisome same.
Actions are poses of will.
Time equivocates then grins,
  Salutes your dull demise,
Your progeny's brief cries

That reach a heaven where
No cunning has tended

And Time has mended
Each woe into fine cloth—
Raiment for a king,
Unruly love undefended.

2. Dylanesque

The river of plenty ran through my heart
Glimmered and glinted till you wrenched it apart.

I trusted your kiss, trusted your touch
Then you said love didn't amount to much,

Was a dog on the street, cloud in the sky,
A wish waiting for time to reply.

You could have been true though who knows when
A man and woman do more than pretend,

Form an angle that's less than oblique,
Or more than a mean blue streak

Through an inner prairie of glass.
I'm flat on my soul's lame ass

Holding a photo that's torn,
Chewing the scraps of your scorn.

We make stuff up, then act like it's real.
That banquet, babe, was my last meal.

Say "Uncle"

How my uncle was a "bachelor"—

                        a word even then,

In the mid-twentieth century, on the way out,

As psychology routed each euphemistic

Behavioral crevice—

               who took women out on "dates"—

Movies (Lana Turner, Liz Taylor), dinner (surf and turf),

Sometimes a touring Broadway play (usually a musical)—

But "nothing ever clicked,"

                   to use my mother's somewhat

Mechanical metaphor, he preferring his own company—

Not that my mother would say that,

                    a little harsh

For her beloved brother but pertaining to the sort

Of metaphysical mothball scent he gave off—

Certitudes kept in the emotional cupboard and never aired

So that Existence became Campbell's soup,

The Cincinnati Reds on the radio, bowling league,

The over-and-over of scores and schedules and carrots

In a tomato broth,

              the starchy brio of tedium,

No one telling you "different," as the Italian family

Down the street liked to put it—

                 which when

I started to read novels made me wonder if

My uncle had some obscure wound beneath

His shield of Midwestern good humor,

                  some silent

Agony that marked him out for inner obloquy,

His days—grading English themes, eating at

A local cafeteria, devotedly watching a few

Tepid sitcoms—seeming strangely insubstantial

Like feathers falling from a great height
And never quite landing yet not airy or soft
But bleak—"that's how it goes" sagacity—
The terror of resignation lodged in a matter-of-fact tone
That must have alerted more than one woman
That he was nonnegotiable, immune to sweet talk,
Incapable of turning the heat up or down
Or giving up his morning gargle of Listerine—
A practice even my mother found "repulsive"—

Yet "what of it?"—
As they used to say all over the neighborhood
Or in my father's words,
"There's no floor plan for the human race,"
All this folk wisdom following me
As I planned how to make my mistakes.

Self-Portrait with Ball

If I had a sense of self, it was a rubber ball
That I was not bouncing or throwing or kicking
But that moved nonetheless would not stay still
But moved away—uncatchable—then came close

Within a hand's reach but veered—uncatchable—
Then fell but bounced hugely—how great I am!—
Only to meet the ceiling of embarrassment and fall
Without grace or pluck and start rolling on the floor

Hither and yon as if seemingly directed pausing
Waiting for me—me?—to say something astute
Like "a ball cannot have a life of its own"—except
Here was the evidence, the first unnameable.

Ode to Worry

Don't worry
Mr. Mrs. Ms. tell me
After I fail the test the bank account the soccer ball
Their chorus implying the opposite message
Advice's reverse spin calling not for
A laissez-faire shrug—you'll get 'em next time kid—
But a wry grimace counseling
Hopeless caution and the power of self-pity
Marshaling several frayed inner boundaries
And thus meshing my abashed psyche
With the specters of out-of-control autos cancers
Tax audits burning smells from hell's kitchen

Did Christ Buddha Mohammad worry?
How petty this noticing
The small change of aggrieved empathy
Pettier than any petty bourgeoisie
Though maybe not maybe the mind turns into
Another overstuffed overheated apartment
So much to hold onto
Dust polish arrange and rearrange and possibly lose
Vases falling off étagères
Cats sneaking into closets and piddling on golf shoes
The jewelry box inviting rubber-soled robbers
While the nation you live in is pillaged too
By rhetoric conceit business-as-usual bribery
While editorialists worry about moral fiber
As if imposing a higher form of breakfast cereal

Don't worry
Which means you can't worry enough
There aren't enough minutes in the fear-diminished day
You don't have enough hands to wring

Why even bother?
Because that's what people do—bother
Themselves and bother others
For good reason for an earring that could fall
Into the bottom of a sink drain
For a love memory ripped out
Of an old notebook and not set on fire
But allowed to flutter in the rampant wind

On Empire

The lawn subdued, machine at rest,
The hero pauses to admire himself:
So much order enforced handily.
The shortened grass enduring.

A small empire but nonetheless
A realm over which an ego
Might tower, not Nero petulant,
But stoic, briefed in care's duties,

Barbarians to meet head on—
The weeds of weeks and circumstance
Waving their ugly, misshapen crowns.
So some patrician once gazed

At the busy slaves loading
And unloading casks of something:
The fecund earth partitioned and ruled,
Lives mowed with brazen, deathly power.

Lament for an Accountant (1959)

Asked about tomorrow's weather, a baseball score,
The latest summit meeting, you would reply,
"It's all about making a buck in America,"
Work being everlasting, the great decipherable sum
You marched with and through and to, as if
A melody were in your head leading you
To another set of books, though not reading books,
Not library books, but books of written figures,
Thick black ledgers of ruled pages
That told the stories, adding up or not,
Cooked or raw, their testimony highlighting
Your ever-twitching left foot, the stolid Pall Mall
Bobbing on pursed lips, ash sprinkled freely,
Cough resonant and dire, the confession
Of one factor among many, slowly but
Steadily erasing you along with the overhead fan
That in the summer "moves the heat around"
Or the galoshes you wore in winter, recalling
Your boyhood and "how much I hated these things."

The calculated days would seem to accrue,
The yellow on your fingers deepening,
Your mutter lengthening when the pluses
And minuses didn't result in a calm balance,
Each measurement, alas, pursuing the daily
Shadow of your ruin. "The world needs us,"
You liked to tell me, as well as "Don't smoke"
And "Women can be serious trouble."
Did you ever smile or laugh? You must have,
Some error encouraging you to forget
Somehow the heartless truth of minute labors,
One long unbirthday, dearth hollering at
Your back to crunch the numbers.

"When I have seen by time's fell hand defaced"

As he lay dying, "some lucid hours"
(His wife told me) were spent memorizing
Shakespeare sonnets that yet haunted him,
His voice feeble (cancer), bitten by pain,
"But present" (she said) "in the play of the sounds."

He'd spent a teacher's lifetime witnessing
Indifference (and worse) to what he cherished
But cleaved steadfastly to what imbued him:
The poet convoking a court where wit was judge
While speaking for and against the wiles of love.

"I'm charming myself," he said lightly to me
In our last phone call. "I've got the feeling of
Something like perfection. Listen," he started
To recite, his voice otherworldly, here
But palpably vanishing, but speaking for
The sake of time's illimitable quickening.

V.

Lyric

"I'll sing the song of love no more," he sang,
Self-conscious and out of tune.

She heard—from a friend of a friend—
And dismissed him again—her voice
Sardonic yet histrionic — "female" he said
When he heard from a friend of a friend
Who slyly winked, as if emotional night
Were stoic day.

He sang some more to the windows, spoons,
And back door while clutching
An urge that refused succor
And blabbed on imperturbably, a sound
She heard from afar and took
As confirmation of what she rued and missed
Yet feared, that rich uncertainty
Spilling over her and him, a tune that
Never knew how to begin.

1893

1. Opium Den

Something hurts, then feints, then hurts.

The soul scowls at the body while
Moments melt to a small sticky ball
But expands too, the rigmarole of clocks
Dissolving into a faintly
　nauseating plenitude.
Oblivion wears a yellow fog
　like a lethal dream,
　like a secret kept captive.

Something hurts, then feints, then hurts.

No government for these spent
　bodies,
Only a sometimes muttered sigh:
Tell me what I should be doing
　now or later
Tell me where I may find
　my purposes
Tell me not to ask myself a question.

Something hurts, then feints, then hurts.

Oh, fall and fall and fall but never hit
　the notion of bottom.
Something bearable in that lethargic spree
But what was there, in faith, to destroy?
The catechism of shoes, meals, and mild intents
　beckoning.

Who asked for these get-along blues?
Who asked these nerves for a parliament?

Something hurts, then feints, then hurts.

2. *Plein Air*

"Paint the light," he urged his charges,
Society women, mostly young, in frocks
But corseted, held in by stays, laces, belts,
Grommets, pins, an extra skeleton
Reforming the loose body whose longings
Emerged in pastels, flicks of a brush, and sighs,
The portent voice of the earth and sky
Calling out, provoking them, as if painting were
Not a sociable accoutrement, something done
To talk of later in amiable, dismissive terms
But a hopelessly felt enchantment that went
Back and forth between them and the gentleman
Artist-teacher squinting and gesticulating
As he strolled amid the darting yet pensive hands,
Muttering encouragement yet halting once in a while
To say nothing, to let some quiet felicity
Sing its unfettered, chromatic heart out.

The Bodyguard

He—it is a largely male occupation—spends time
Waiting in cars where under the pale
Interior light he reads long novels by women.

His boss, a quiet preoccupied executive,
Has never asked him a question about himself
As a human being.

That is okay.

His feelings are not hurt.

He is free to move from one page to another
Like a snail or beetle.
His admittedly pudgy fingers meditatively
Considering the textures of design.

"Women give it away," other men have told him,
And in the novels there is
A scrap of truth to that saying.
Things are said about longings and confusions
That did not have to be said,
That could have stayed in the bureau drawer
With the hairbrushes, lotions, and scarves.

He lifts weights, goes for long walks
With Gus, his golden retriever, has been dating a woman
For three years.

They circle around one another
Like fish, then they hunger, then they circle again.

Out in the distance someone is ready to kill his boss.

He must be ready to die and thinks about it now and then
While idling at a light
Or starting up the car in the morning.

Is that what men know?

He wants to ask his lover
What she thinks but is ashamed.

He consults another page.
A woman in an apartment is shouting
Into a telephone after a man has hung up.

Time for his boss to be leaving the building.

The bodyguard exhales.

His breath lingers in the air,
Palpable as a plum or a peach.

He dreams about unwariness and he
Wants to embrace her.

Herr Plath Doktor

To resurrect the grave of your head
  I attach these electrodes
    To flay the fear within you

I chant some words
  Die little mind snakes
    Let the sky within you breathe

The shitstorm of bent science
  Imposture but faith desperate faith
    Something to be done with this long crazy phase

Your insistent desire to die
  Before the sanctioned time
    Your clanking protuberant love-caught heart

Your sincerely sanctimonious tears
  Something to be done

    This apparatus vanquishes the shades

This unmetered force unnerves all wishes
  Lifts your bleak mental skin
    Sends you into a bright no-place

Where with some practice—
  "Hello, I feel okay today
    How are you? How are you? How are you?"

Zap! Like a comic book
  Your mouth expands your hair jumps
    Zap! You lose your past

But memories only breed remorse
　　It's better this way some purity
　　　　Careening through you cleaning you out

Leaving you fresh brittle empty
　　Clear as some mythical pond
　　　　Where passion forgets and joy shrieks

Recalling Sophocles

Gradually
     the days
         grew dark.
Our faces
     turned
         inside out.
The animals
     spoke
         to us
Dire
   and terse
       with warning.
We
   who dismissed tragedy
         and pushed
Doom aside
     as we
         doomed others
Could not
     stare
        in any mirror,
Our only
     echo being
        a ruined voice
On a long-
     ago stage,
         lamenting
His blindness
     and seeing
         too late
How *human*
     was
       fate.

"I Have Themistocles the Athenian"

Midwinter, radiators ticking, clanking,
Now and then whistling a wisp of steam,
On the living-room sofa an old man reading
Plutarch in the Dryden/Clough translation,
A Harvard Classic published in 1909
By P. F. Collier & Son, a little
Yellowed, bookish history right there
In his veined, age-splotched hands, the paper
Crisp but not brittle or worm-eaten, still
The path to Pericles, Themistocles,
Alcibiades, ancient worthies, sometime tricksters,
Loci of virtue and contention, ministers
Of tribal politics, debaters, warriors,
Their lucid, internecine doings a legacy shoved
Down many a collegian throat as the male grandeur
Of unrepentant, metal-forging civilization:
"Having made himself master of the port,
He laid siege to the Samians," et cetera.
So he finds himself comfortably
Collapsing within the folds of copious sentences,
Rereading paragraphs, lingering on dependent
Clauses, an intricacy of articulation
Giving a bass note to measure and counter-
Measure, every victory or defeat expanding
Fame's borders while the barbarians lapped
At the gilded, bloody shore demanding their
Undue share of wearying, heroic vigilance.

Light snow for days, the maples furred and blobbed,
Delicately rimed, while the annals beckon
A later man to lay down his struggling arms

And heed the declarations and motives,
The scritch-scratch of ardent voices on
Perishable air, a ravenous eloquence
Asking only to be obeyed.

Pandemic, Nursing Home, Wisconsin, November, 2020

Listen—
Thin voices among metal cabinets doors low
Ceilings wheelchairs ceramic tiles ventilator
Ducts linoleum plastic cups thermometers
The material-all-too-much, chatting, fretting,
Beseeching.

How did Master Death come to be here?
Who in the round of duties invited him?
He must have, he could have, he did,
He let himself in through an open window
One summer day, pretending he was young
And then not leaving, discarding all verb tenses,
Squatting at the entrance and examining
Each spare, unspeculative day,
Eating what he ate yesterday, the gruel of fortune
Amid a wan eternity of wavering spoons
Lifted to modest mouths, the beaks of fledglings
Marooned, abandoned to this singleness,
The body, a mass of perimeters, stubborn yet weak,
While pills and fears prowl the hallways
Peering in the rooms that are the same rooms
Filled with the same perhaps lethal spirit
The same moans and stares that linger on a face
Gone seventy years yet terribly near.

The History Hotel

October. Someone lays a wreath on the derelict porch
   of the History Hotel.
Shutters bang in the long-standing breeze.
The wreath layer thinks: This is for Aunt Laura and her dog, Hansi,
Known only in a photo from 1933 in which Laura
   perches on a rocker
And looks pensively at the camera
   while at her feet Hansi sits obediently
   waiting in that way dogs wait,
Understanding how time is empty and full and may offer a biscuit.
Word was that Laura had been "a maiden aunt."

October, the season of dying disappointments,
Beloved of gravediggers, poets, and dog walkers.

Later, someone else comes along and wonders
   who laid the wreath,
And how come the hotel from who-knows-when
   is still standing.
Is it a memorial? Did destiny get lost? That patina—
   is it regret or verdigris?

A dog sniffs the abundant leaf litter.

October—you can feel time running down, the race run.
Will this happen to *me*?
More to the point, will it happen to *you*?
Yes, but not worth thinking about. Better
   to straighten the wreath.
Better to call the dog's name to which the dog answers
With that eagerness that makes memory sob.

ACKNOWLEDGMENTS

Thanks to the editors of the following publications in which these poems first appeared, sometimes in different forms:

American Journal of Poetry: "And You, Thomas Hardy" (as "Thomas Hardy"), "Ode to Worry," "On Empire" (as "The Yard Man"), "Recalling Sophocles" (as "Concerning the Evidence")

Beltway Poetry Quarterly: "Brief," "Dog Is My Copilot" (as "*Dasein*"), "For Raymond Lévy," "Lament for an Accountant (1959)," "A Memorable Occasion: Opening the Doors," "The New Wave," "NFL Poem (Annals of Male Americana)," "Night, Apartment Towers, Manhattan," "Self-Portrait with Ball," "Selfie"

The Bollman Bridge Review: "A Certain Teacher Does Some Banking" (as "Renfrew Does Some Banking")

The Hudson Review: "Elegy for the Poet Adam Zagajewski"

I-70: "Hopperesque"

Limberlost Review: "The Bodyguard"

The Manhattan Review: "Aces" (as "The Writer Dostoevsky"), "The History Hotel," "1910," "Now and then it rains money," "Ode to the Stock Exchange," "Upon the Death of the Actor Philip Seymour Hoffman from 'Acute Drug Intoxication'"

Vox Populi: "Once," "The Shuffle"

"Dylanesque" first appeared in *Visiting Bob: Poems Inspired by the Life and Work of Bob Dylan,* edited by Thom Tammaro and Alan Davis (New Rivers Press, 2018). "Sentence" first appeared in *The Golden Shovel Anthology,* edited by Peter Kahn, Ravi Shankar, and Patricia Smith (University of Arkansas Press, 2017, 2019). "On a Foreseen Death, August 4, 1962" first appeared in *I Wanna Be Loved by You: Poems on Marilyn Monroe,* edited by Susana H. Case and Margo Taft Stever (Milk & Cake Press, 2022).

CAVANKERRY'S MISSION

A not-for-profit literary press serving art and community, CavanKerry is committed to expanding the reach of poetry and other fine literature to a general readership by publishing works that explore the emotional and psychological landscapes of everyday life, and to bringing that art to the underserved where they live, work, and receive services.

OTHER BOOKS IN THE NOTABLE VOICES SERIES

An Apron Full of Beans: New and Selected Poems, Sam Cornish
The Poetry Life: Ten Stories, Baron Wormser
BEAR, Karen Chase
Fun Being Me, Jack Wiler
Common Life, Robert Cording
The Origins of Tragedy & Other Poems, Kenneth Rosen
Apparition Hill, Mary Ruefle
Against Consolation, Robert Cording

The History Hotel was typeset in Arno Pro, which was created by Robert Slimbach at Adobe. The name refers to the river that runs through Florence, Italy.